To Bruce Warren and his cats

All illustrations by Jasper Burns (Some illustrations used courtesy of Virginia Museum of Natural History and MacMillan Travel.)

Published by:

Pietas Publications
Waynesboro, Virginia, USA
web: www.jasperburns.com
email: pietas@jasperburns.com

ANIMAL OBITUARIES

By Jasper Burns

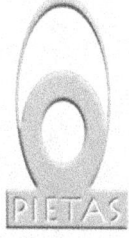

ANIMAL OBITUARIES

CONTENTS

PREFACE

There is an unimaginable number of living beings on the earth at any given moment. The number of animals alone has been estimated at 20 quintillion (billion billion) individuals. Are the lives of some creatures more valuable than others? For example, do animal lives matter less than human lives? Day for day, year for year, do wild animals live less eventful or less important lives than human beings?

As humans, we tend to believe that our lives are intrinsically more precious and significant. But on what is this presumption of human superiority based?

For some, it is a matter of religious belief; that animals have no souls or that humans have been given ascendancy by God, despite the fact that many humans have succumbed to "lower forms of life".

Ideas of human superiority may be based on superior size or longevity, even though many animals are larger than humans and some live longer - and the fact that we don't value smaller or short-lived humans less.

The claim of human superiority is sometimes based on human accomplishments, talents, skills, knowledge, and material acquisitions that are beyond the scope of animals. However, all animals have capabilities and experiences that are beyond the scope of humans – and we do not discount the lives of human infants or the disabled because they are lacking in accomplishments, knowledge, or abilities.

If the value of a life may be shown by how vigorously a creature fights to preserve it, then anyone who has spent an hour trying to kill a fly knows that he values his life just as highly as any human – and is at least as alert and aware of his self-interest. All animals and humans possess consciousness, which cannot be subdivided; a creature either has it and is alive or does not have it and is dead – or in deep sleep.

Many or most humans think of themselves as having a destiny. They expect their lives to have highs and lows - changes of fortune brought about by their choices and/or fate. By comparison, animal lives may seem less rich and less meaningful. However, few people have any sustained experience of the lives of wild animals; most impressions are based on the observation of domesticated pets and livestock. These lives are analogous to those of children and of adults who are incarcerated in prisons or institutions. Domesticated animals are not allowed to make significant life choices. Many are denied the opportunity to reproduce or to choose or compete for mates. They are not allowed to live as independent beings and so their lives are controlled and limited.

One crude measure of a human life is the obituary. It gives a summary of an individual's experiences, family connections, accomplishments, characteristics, and interests. Obituaries have occasionally been written for animals and even plants who have achieved fame in the human world – famous redwoods, racehorses, dog actors, animal astronauts, and circus performers have received their due. Many of us could write some sort of biography for our pets.

Scientists who study animal behavior may construct generalized life histories that give insights into the lives of animals. However, a generalized life history of a human being would have little value for describing an individual's life experience and the same is true for animals.

The following pages contain a series of imagined but fact-based animal obituaries. They are written in fundamentally human terms – few attempts are made to describe their subject's thoughts or feelings or those of their animal associates as these are beyond human understanding. However, the basic facts – the family connections, places of residence, activities and accomplishments - may give a sense of the lives that were lived, and of their value.

The deceased have been given names. This may seem anomalous for wild creatures. However, naming is a human convention that helps us recognize the unique character and value of each individual – a courtesy that animals also deserve.

THE OBITUARIES

GREGORY THE GREAT BLUE HERON
(Ardea herodias)

It was with sadness that I heard this week of the passing of an old friend: Gregory, the Great Blue Heron of Blue Spruce Lake. I have known Old Greg since he was a nestling 17 years ago. I live in a cabin on the lake, just about a mile and a half from the heronry where he was born and so I was able to keep track of him all through the years.

Greg spent winters elsewhere; I always liked to picture him in Jamaica or someplace like that, soaking up the sun while I was shivering under three feet of snow. But he always came back in springtime and I watched from a distance every year as he chose a nesting site, found a mate, and raised his brood. He spent most of each day on the eggs till they hatched – his mate took the night shift – and they both brought food to the chicks, regurgitating all the fish and frogs and gophers the young birds could eat.

Yes, Gregory was a fine bird; as tall (four foot two) and handsome a heron as you'll ever see, but that's not why I'll miss him. You see, he was my teacher. I learned more from that bird than from any human teacher I ever had. And all I had to do was watch him. Greg was so focused, so patient, so brave. Maybe those are clichés for a heron, but you'd have to spend thousands of hours watching him like I did to really know what I mean.

I used to go into a trance sometimes, watching him meditate on a fish – keeping his head as still as stone while his reed-like legs imperceptibly inched his body forward. Then his head would follow so gracefully it lulled you - and the fish - to sleep. But if the fish moved away, it didn't bother old Greg. He'd just start over with a new one. Greg never got frustrated - and he never gave up.

What a sight it was to see Gregory glide across the sky. The great wing beats seemed to soothe the clouds and tickle the pine needles. Always took my breath away. Again, so slow and graceful and patient. But Greg could be quick as lightning, too. When he had the range on a gopher or a brook trout, no eye could follow his strike. It seemed like he never missed, but he did, and, when he did, he didn't mind. He never gave up.

And so he taught me patience and one-pointedness and persistence – and how to let go of broken dreams. But he taught me more than that.

When he was 11, I watched him defend his nest from a bald eagle. The raptor could have crushed his skull with her talons, or ripped out his heart with her beak – and she would eat a full-grown heron as readily as a chick. But Greg wouldn't give an inch. He spread his wings and croaked defiantly, stabbing his dagger bill at the larger bird repeatedly until the eagle was bleeding and had had enough. I learned courage that day. I learned that sometimes you just don't back down, no matter what the odds.

And so Greg is gone now. But I will never forget what he taught me about life and strength and dignity. I have a little shrine to him in my bedroom – a photo I took of him, a feather he lost last summer, an empty egg shell that dropped from his nest. But the shrine that will last longest is in my heart.

Those who wish to honor Gregory's memory may make donations to The Blue Heron Nature Preserve.

CLOVER SPOT THE EASTERN BOX TURTLE
(Terrapene carolina)

Died March 30, 2006, aged 102, Clover Spot. She was born on October 3, 1903 in Fluvanna County, Virginia beneath a tulip poplar tree. Her mother was Split Shell and her father was either Two Toe or Orange Eye, both of whom knew her mother well.

At the age of twelve minutes, Clover Spot saw three of her four siblings eaten by a crow. However, she and her brother Corn Bill scampered under a fallen log and were saved.

When she was 4, Clover Spot was moved by a human being to Richmond, Virginia, where she lived for a time before escaping and gradually making her way to the Drover Creek Valley. Her first children were born there, though by the time her eggs had hatched Clover Spot was living in a garage in Lynchburg, Virginia, having been carried there by a truck driver as a gift for his niece.

It was at this time that Clover Spot became seriously malnourished to the point of losing consciousness. She was moved by trash truck to the Campbell County landfill, where she eventually regained her senses and dined on enough worms, cockroaches, and food scraps to restore her strength. She spent the winter in an old bathtub and was inadvertently carried to the vicinity of the Staunton River near Brookneal, Virginia where she spent many of her happiest years.

When she turned eighty, Clover Spot was mauled by a hunting dog and lost the use of her right eye. The hunter carved his initials on her shell and then released her in the Blue Ridge Mountains, where she was pestered by skunks and raccoons and even a bear. Living was hard in the highlands, so she followed a stream down into the Shenandoah Valley where she spent the remainder of her days, finally passing away from dehydration in an old chicken coop where some children had kept and then forgotten her.

Clover Spot was extremely fond of blackberries and snails. She enjoyed a gentle rain and the first worm of spring. She is survived by three children, fourteen grandchildren, fifty-six great grandchildren, two hundred and six great-great grandchildren, and an undetermined number of more remote descendants. Her remains are scattered in several places in the Wilsons' back yard. In lieu of flowers, friends may make donations to the National Save the Sea Turtle Foundation.

LAUREN THE LOCUST BORER BEETLE
(Megacyllene robiniae)

Who will mourn for Lauren the beetle? Even at birth she was labelled a pestilence, a plague, a scourge. She was the dreaded "round-headed borer", the sinister white grub munching a black locust tree, tunneling beneath the bark, into the sapwood and even the heartwood, leaving tell-tale mounds of white and yellow sawdust. After pupating inside the tree, she would emerge as a furry black and yellow beetle that looked like a yellow-jacket. Then she would fly off to find another innocent locust tree and lay her eggs in its cuts and scars and the parasitic cycle would go on.

From Lauren's perspective, however, life was a year-long feast without evil intentions. After the long dark months chewing through her tree, she emerged to fly and frolic with her kind, tasting sun and sex and Goldenrod pollen until a deep freeze ended her brief career. It was a peaceful existence. There were enemies – woodpeckers and wheel bugs ate most of her siblings before they were grown, and human beings waged chemical warfare against her, but she completed her cycle and died fulfilled.

Humans value black locust trees because they give shade and will grow in poor, damaged soil, where farming and strip mining and housebuilding and other human activities have stripped away or compacted the earth. But humans don't like the way locusts grow into thorny, impenetrable thickets, which protect the trees and wild animals and plants. Humans like locusts to grow into tall trees with single trunks that ornament and shade their lawns, so they prune them – they cut their branches and the sap bleeds.

Locust Borers and Locust Trees are old friends, you see. They have lived together for millions of years. The beetles attack the trees that are sickly or injured – or have been pruned. They cull the weak and strengthen the locust herd, like lions do for wildebeests and cougars do or did for deer. Like tree doctors and nurses, the adult beetles inspect the locust trees, looking for the weak and dying and treating their wounds with eggs – the seeds of a new generation of tree doctors and nurses. And so the cycle continues – unless the new-coming humans find a better poison.

So perhaps it is the locust trees who will mourn for Lauren?

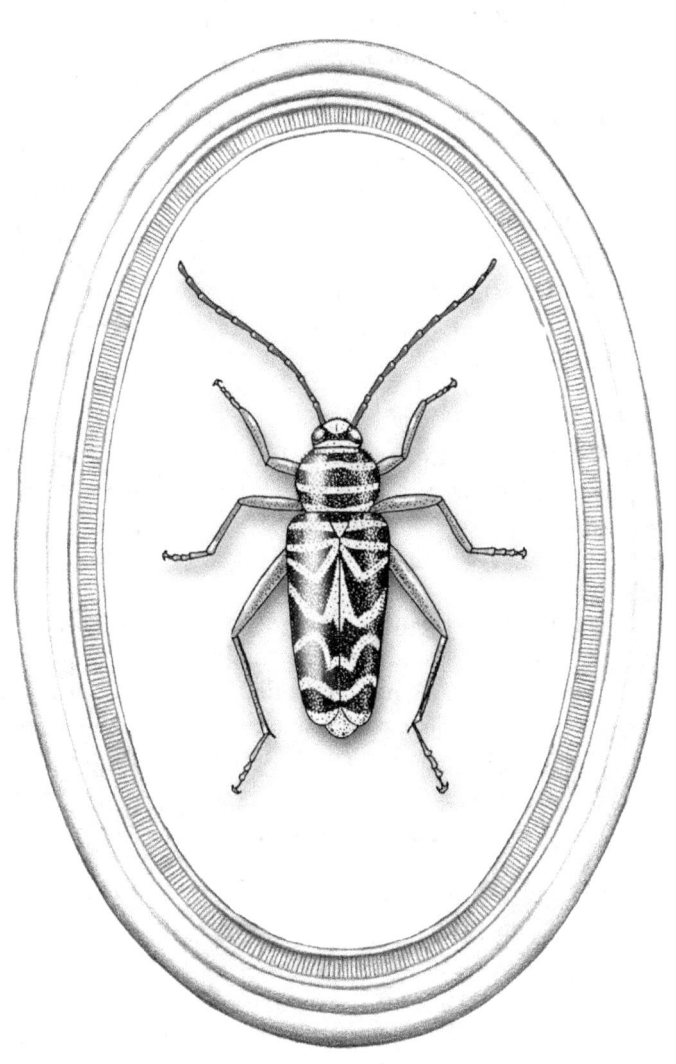

STELLA THE MUD DAUBER
(Sceliphron caementarium)

One's first impression of Stella might have been a negative one. She was a wasp, after all, with a long slender black and yellow body and a needle-thin waist. Her hindquarters tapered to a sharp and shiny point and, yes, it contained a stinger, which doubled as an egg-laying tube. She looked wicked, sure enough, which was a good thing for her because people usually stayed far away. But Stella was a gentle wasp. You'd really have to bother her a lot to make her use her weapon, and her sting wasn't nearly as painful as a hornet's, or a yellow jacket's, or even a bee's.

She spent the daylight hours alone, visiting flowers in the fields and gardens where she drank her fill of nectar. Sometimes Stella even visited hummingbird feeders. Her nights were spent sleeping in a bush, often with several other mud daubers.

When nest-building began, Stella spent a lot of time at puddles in search of the mud she needed for construction. The nest grew into a ball-shaped mass of two dozen thick-walled cylindrical cells, each one stuffed with spiders that she had caught in the fields and paralyzed with her stinger. Then she laid an egg in each cell and sealed it up. When all were provisioned and sealed, Stella moved on to spend her final days sipping nectar, dying at the age of one year and seven days.

Stella had lived a simple, inoffensive life, but she left a dramatic, unexpected mark on history. She had made her nest in the air speed measurement tube of a Boeing 757. No one noticed, and the blockage caused the jet to crash, killing 189 people. Ironically, all of her offspring had died before this happened – eaten by cuckoo wasp larvae who had hatched in the nest and were finishing off the paralyzed spiders when the crash occurred.

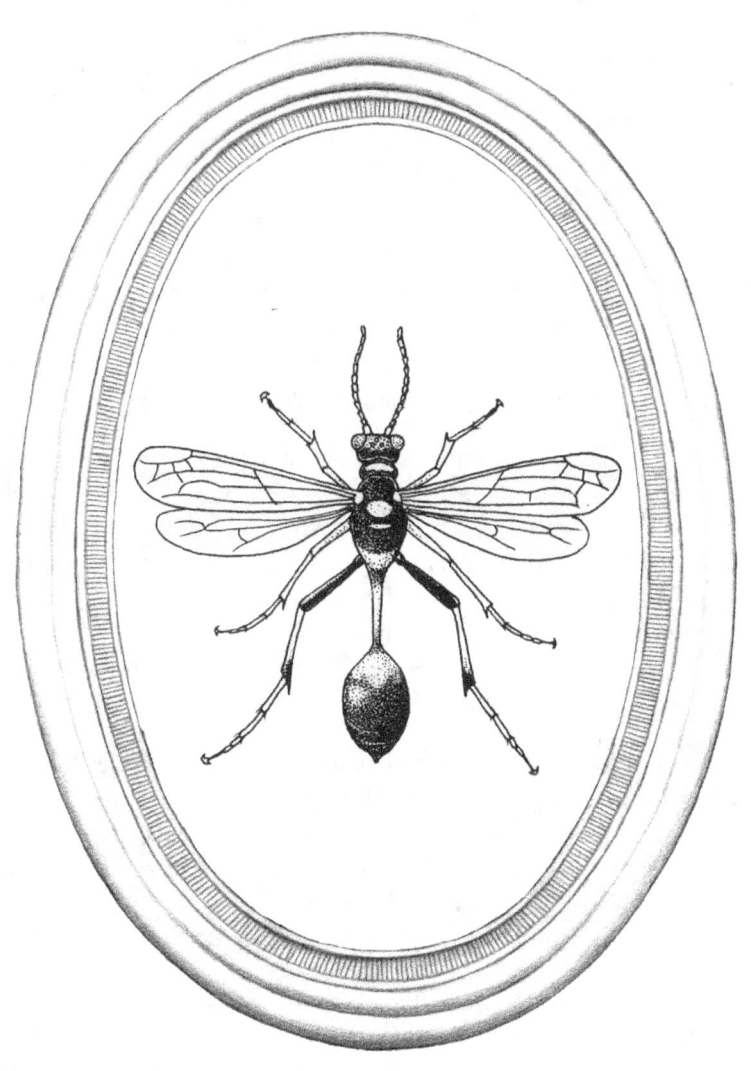

GRAWP THE LARGEMOUTH BASS
(Micropterus salmoides)

How can words do justice to the grandeur of Grawp, the storied behemoth of Deep Gorge Lake? He died Thursday night at the age of 24, though some won't believe it and will continue to imagine him patrolling the murky depths.

He was a loner, deeply scarred by an early near-death experience when he found himself inside a Great Blue Heron. Fortunately, the bird had swallowed a thorny twig along with Grawp and had to vomit him out. Grawp made good his escape and, ever after, preferred deep water, avoiding the shallows except to mate and raise his young.

He was the father of more than 960,000 small fry, whom he dutifully and intrepidly protected during their first weeks of life. He was popular with egg-layers for the perfect round nests he scooped out of the mud and his gentle courtships. Eventually, his unmatched size and strength were the greatest persuaders of all and females queued up to deposit their eggs in his nurseries. Even though Grawp ate almost 1500 of his own children during their adolescence and adulthood, he is survived today by more than 20,000 descendants.

Grawp was a giant among freshwater fish, nearly two feet long and weighing almost 10 pounds in his later years – a size almost unprecedented for a male of his species. Many will remember his grace and majesty as he cruised beneath the water lily mats in search of birds, his favorite prey. How fitting that his last meal was a plump Mallard duckling - to which an ambitious angler had attached a treble hook.

Grawp had been seldom hooked and never landed before in his lifetime, but he was well-known to local fishermen. Many had seen his shadowy form move into deeper water on their approach. They didn't know that he rarely fed during the day.

Needless to say, Abner Festus of Wilcox, Mississippi was suitably awed by his catch. After taking several photographs, he rushed to return Grawp to his kingdom. Alas, the hook had been swallowed and the mighty fish passed into legend.

Admirers of the deceased may send tokens of respect to the National Fish and Wildlife Foundation.

TUKTU THE CARIBOU
(Rangifer tarandus)

From the beginning, Tuktu was a prodigy. He weighed 20 pounds at birth – a full 7 pounds above average. By the age of 12 months, he was already as tall and heavy as most of the grown males and he was so quick and strong that he won the right to mate in his very first mature season, at the age of only one and a half. By his second year, he could leap higher, run faster, and fight longer than any other buck in the herd. His vast antlers inspired awe and trembling. He was a super-caribou, so all were saddened when he passed away this week at the relatively young age of nine.

Tuktu took great pleasure in displaying his strength and agility. He was like a buck among fawns during rutting season. In fact, in his prime, Tuktu's battles were almost won before they began. His opponents knew that their only chance of success was a lucky first jab before Tuktu had set himself. Failing in that, they faced a hopeless test of strength and antler size that they could not win. Fortunately for them, Tuktu was not vindictive, never injuring an opponent after victory was assured.

There are many stories about Tuktu's appetite. It is said that he could strip all the leaves from a birch sapling in less than a minute and gobble down ten pounds of lichen in a single meal. His weight generally hovered around 600 pounds by early fall – almost all muscle, bone, and rock-hard antler.

But as remarkable as Tuktu's physical gifts were, he will not be remembered for them alone. His courage and self-sacrifice at the end of his life will ensure his place in the hearts and memories of all who witnessed his valiant last stand.

A grizzly bear with two cubs ambushed the vanguard of the herd by the river bank on Tuesday evening. A young doe was wounded and unable to run. Though he was quite some distance from the bears and on the other side of the river, Tuktu bounded into the water and lodged himself between the adult bear and the wounded doe.

The grizzly rushed towards Tuktu and tore open his left front leg. Tuktu didn't flinch. He set his hooves in the gravel and lowered his mighty rack, thwarting every charge as the bear feinted and lunged. The struggle lasted for almost half an hour. By the end, both bear and caribou were bleeding and snorting for breath. Finally the grizzly managed to plant a heavy paw on Tuktu's shoulder and push him off his feet. The fight was soon over, but the herd, including the lame doe, were safely away.

Tuktu is survived by numerous descendants from seven generations. Those who wish to honor his life and heroism may do so with a contribution to Defenders of Wildlife.

ORPHEA THE OSPREY
(Pandion haliaetus)

She was born on top of a piling in the Chesapeake Bay and had just left her home waters for her 22nd annual flight to Brazil when she ran into a violent squall and was blown into rough water. She struggled to regain flight, but the wind was too strong. Exhausted, she drowned at sea; her remains being shared by sea gulls and blue crabs.

When she was three, Orphea met her life partner, Deiphon. Together, they raised 12 groups of nestlings before Deiphon was killed by a Bald Eagle while defending the nest. Orphea refused to mate that year or the next, but she accepted another partner, Cirrus, the following spring.

Orphea preferred fishing in brackish water and savored perch above other species, though she never rejected any easy prey. She once tackled a four pound flounder near Cape Hatteras. The fish was so cumbersome that it took her a full five minutes to become airborne again – by which time she had drawn the attention of a hammerhead shark. Her escape was of the narrowest variety.

She was less fortunate on another occasion when a large catfish she had pulled from a river in Cuba managed to stab her with its pectoral spine as she carried it to a perch. The wound to the base of her talon was deep and became infected. For a time, she could not fish and it seemed she would perish, but Orphea sustained herself on carrion and managed to recover.

She was an excellent mother – her gold-ringed eyes always watching for danger. She provided fish for her nestlings so well that only a few of them died of hunger. One year, Orphea and Deiphon nested in a dead pine tree along the shore and a raccoon managed to reach her eggs while she was on duty. She fought valiantly against the beast, finally driving him away after losing but one egg and sustaining only minor injuries.

Many of Orphea's children and grandchildren continue to spend the warmer months in the Chesapeake Bay area. Therefore, friends may wish to contribute to the Chesapeake Bay Foundation.

CHAN-CHAN THE BOA CONSTRICTOR
(Boa constrictor)

Chan-chan the six foot boa has died at his home in Brooklyn at the age of 17. He passed away sometime in the past few weeks – no one is quite sure when because no one had seen him move for a while. When told that Chan-chan had passed away, his caretaker Bernie replied, "Oh yeah? How can you tell?"

Bernie had been keeping Chan-chan in a large aquarium for just over four years. At first, he was fascinated with his pet snake, keeping his water fresh and regularly providing him with rats and guinea pigs and even the occasional bunny.

But then Bernie's new girlfriend Kirstie moved in. She disapproved of Chan-chan and Bernie gradually lost interest. Chan-chan's hairy feces and chalky urine began to pile up. The water bowl was either half-full of milky muck or empty. Then the lady at the corner pet store stopped selling rats to Bernie when she found out what he was doing with them. It was a pain to go across town to the other pet store, so feedings became scarce. Bernie knew boas could go a long time without food, and Chan-chan still looked pretty good. He was shocked to feel the dead snake's ribs and hollow belly. Probable cause of death: starvation.

It was a sad ending to an eventful life that began in the Panama jungle. Chan-chan was one of 32 snakelings born to his mother in the shade of a banana tree. Some were full siblings; others only half, but it didn't matter because Chan-chan left the brood immediately after wriggling free from his mother and never saw any of them again. He swam across the Rio Teribe and climbed into the 3-dimensional labyrinth of the forest, living on birds and lizards and drinking water from leaf-lined pools in tree elbows high above the ground.

By the time he was three and almost five feet long, he was spending most of his time on the forest floor, avidly pursuing females whose scent trails thrilled and energized him. Chan-chan was most active at night. Lacking ears, he was oblivious to the insect racket but his forked tongue tasted the surroundings and he could "see" the warmth of prey and foe with his lip sensors. He spent most of the daylight hours motionless.

Chan-chan was eleven years old when his jungle began to be cleared. Food became scarce and females even scarcer, so he followed the river downstream. He floated past human settlements and had a near escape from an angry dog who couldn't swim quite as fast as he could. Finally, he moved into the crawl space under a storage shed next to a fish market, feasting on the rats that swarmed under the building. Then one chilly morning, he emerged to sun himself on the dock. A young boy grasped Chan-chan's tail, dodged his open-mouthed strikes, and thrust him into an empty grain sack.

Thus began Chan-chan's journey through a series of import stores and pet shops that finally brought him to Bernie. Donations may be made in Chan-chan's memory to The Humane Society.

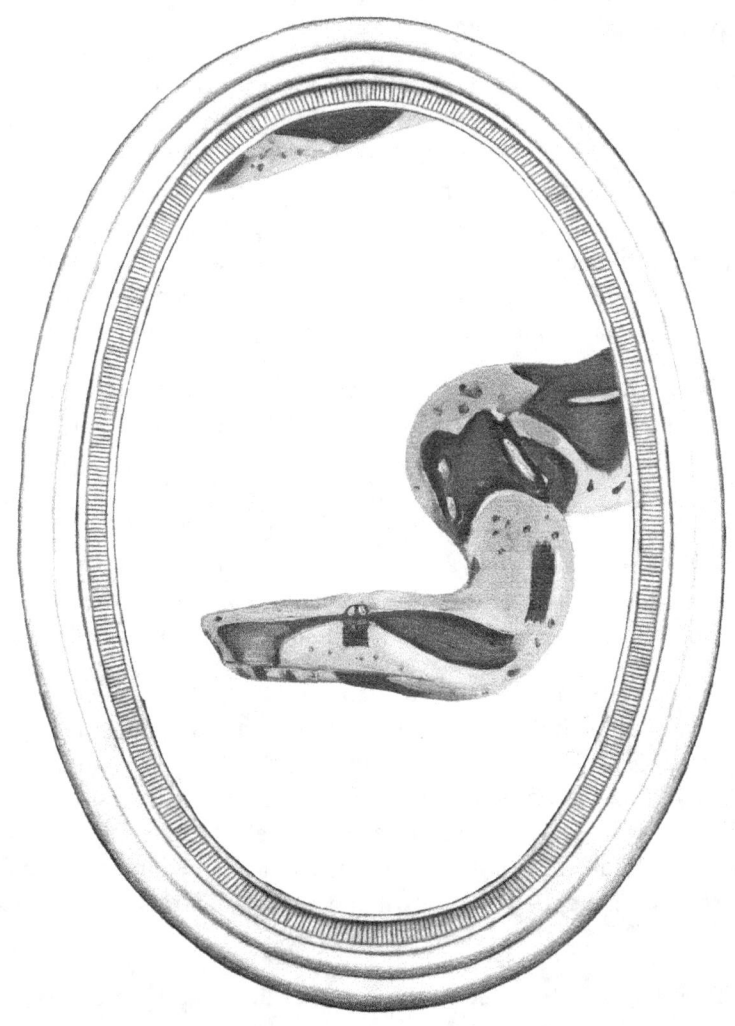

ARCHIE THE HAWKSBILL TURTLE
(Eretmochelys imbricata)

Archie was used to being followed – by fish of all colors, shapes, and sizes. Also by those strange creatures with glass eyes and long legs and flippers who shone lights in his face and belched up bubbles. But Sunday he was pursued by something much larger; something that was more than curious. A giant shark bit down on his carapace with such force that it buckled. Archie's insides trailed behind him as he spiraled down, bludgeoned repeatedly as the shark tore off his limbs and then his head. It was a sudden and violent end to a long and peaceful life spent cruising tropical seas and coral reefs, munching on sponges and anemones, taking it slow and easy.

Archie was hatched 56 years ago on a quiet Mexican beach with more than a hundred siblings. They scurried over the sand toward the water as quickly as their tiny flippers could carry them, but Archie and one of his sisters were scooped up by a sea gull. Fortunately for him, the gull was too greedy and dropped Archie into the sea. It was the lucky beginning of a charmed life. True, there were difficult moments. Hurricanes and fishing nets could be tedious. And there was time spent in the city aquarium until a fungal infection forced them to let him go.

It seemed he was in no hurry to grow up – Archie first mated at the age of 23. He gripped the front of her shell with his clawed flippers and rode her back as she swam slowly near the water's surface. Occasionally, he had to wrestle another turtle out of his territory, biting and grappling plastron to plastron, flipping each other over until one of them gave way. But he saw fewer and fewer turtles as the years went by. That suited him well most of the time; fewer turtles meant more sponges. But finding females when he wanted them grew difficult.

For some of us, Archie's life might seem uneventful; even boring. But we shouldn't judge without having swum a few thousand miles in his shell. He lived in a warm, colorful world, where many things were edible and few could bother him. He felt the steady caress of the sea and could swim and dive as effortlessly as an albatross can fly. He could take a few hours' nap on the bottom when he wanted to and taste the sweet air when he needed to. Most of the time, his stress level was near zero.

Those who wish to see Archie's way of life continue may wish to make a contribution to the Sea Turtle Conservancy.

LUNA THE MOTH
(Actias luna)

It was a brief but successful life that ended Tuesday. Luna's magnificent pale green wings had been reduced to shreds and tatters by the wind and hard work and a close call with a screech owl. And she hadn't eaten or drunk water in eight days. She was exhausted.

Only two months ago, Luna the egg was laid by her mother on the bottom of a sweet gum leaf. She hatched, wandered around a bit, and then started munching. She was very good at munching.

Luna grew rapidly. Every week or so, she needed to shed her skin and graduate to the next level of caterpillar. Her form changed, but munching leaves remained her occupation. It was a pleasant life, clutching the midrib of a leaf and filling up on green stuff. When it rained, she moved underneath and held on as the droplets pounded her green umbrella.

For the first few weeks, Luna had stayed closed to her siblings, but then they went their separate ways. When she moved on, it was with a long slow gallop, her many legs flowing forward, each pair in unison.

And then she hardened into a pupa under a rock and waited for the big change. A baby skunk found her glistening red-brown shell and bounced her around a bit, but Luna spun her pointy tail like a wasp sting and the skunk lost its nerve.

What a thrill and surprise it must have been to burst forth and have wings! She unfurled them slowly, let them dry, then she flew off to find a mate. Fortunately, he was looking for her, too. Their soft white furry bodies pressed together as they dangled from a branch. And then she was off; there was no time to waste.

You see, adult Luna moths have no mouths; they can't eat or drink, so their days are numbered and their energy finite. And there was much to do; such as laying 500 eggs on the undersides of leaves, half a dozen at a time, while avoiding bats and toads and cats – and bright artificial lights.

Luna fulfilled her mission. She cast off her tattered husk and died, survived by hundreds of tiny green caterpillars.

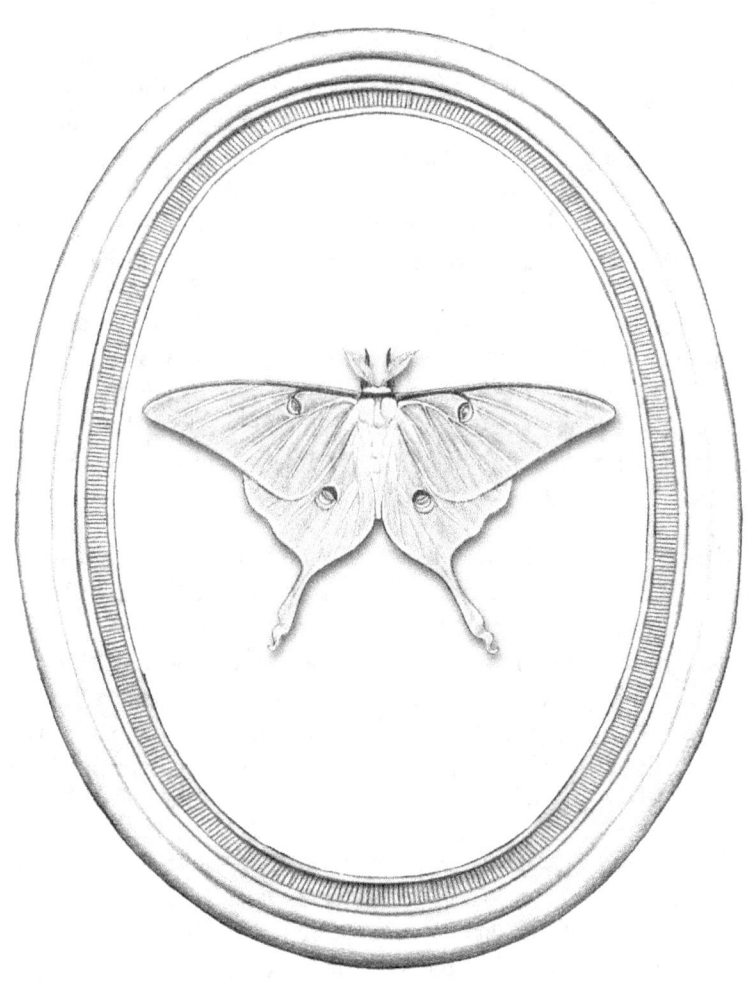

FORINA THE FIRE ANT
(Solenopsis mandibularis)

An active and valuable citizen of the Mesquite by the Dry Stream Colony, Forina was born during difficult times. A lingering drought had made seeds and green plants scarce, and the 250,000 inhabitants were on close rations. The wells of the nest were constantly being extended deeper to reach the water table and the foragers went so far afield in search of food that many never found their way back.

After pupating, Forina worked in the nursery for two months and then moved into the chamber of one of the queens. It was here that she was happiest, deep in the heart of the mound with its countless rooms and tunnels. Though she could not see anything in the darkness, the rich fragrance of pheromones permeated her being and kept her oriented and connected.

When she was three months old, Forina joined the foraging crew, working initially as a gatherer. What a shock it was the first time she emerged from the safety of the mound and saw the searing sunlight and felt the pulsing wind! At first she carried bits of food that were brought by foragers into the larder, but she soon learned to follow the scent trails some distance from the mound, where she helped retrieve seeds and dead insects. However, none of this prepared her for the excitement of hunting live prey.

Her first quarry was a garden spider on open ground. She and several hundred of her sisters climbed onto the gigantic creature and held on for dear life as it thrashed and shuddered in desperation. Stung and bitten countless times, the spider slowed and then died. The triumphant ants tore the spider into tiny bits and carried them to the mound.

Forina's later encounters included a horned lizard, two snakes, a wounded sparrow, and several grasshoppers. All of these were vanquished, but the colony still remained hard-pressed to feed itself. In fact, the queens had to reduce their rates of reproduction because there simply wasn't enough food. The colony began to die.

By this time, Forina knew so much about the surrounding terrain and was so experienced in foraging techniques, that she became a scout and teacher of younger ants. She would blaze and mark new pheromone trails and became one of the colony's best providers. Still, it wasn't enough to reverse the dying trend.

Then Forina gave her last and greatest service to her community. Alone, she wandered farther than any ant had ever ventured from the mound. Risking dehydration and almost out of range of the colony's scent, she came upon a strangely frozen river of a sticky black substance that seemed to be a trail for huge metal beasts that zoomed by and blew her into the brush – where she found the half-eaten remains of a Happy Meal.

Spending her dwindling reserves in laying down the pheromone trail and carrying a sample morsel home, Forina struggled back to the mound. Night fell, and still she was far from the colony. The next morning, she finally stumbled onto a busy trailhead and followed it to the edge of the mound, where she collapsed, so depleted that she couldn't move. It was there that she died, aged sixteen and a half months. The burger and fries Forina had found helped sustain the colony until the rains came.

Those who wish to make a charitable donation in Forina's honor are out of luck – no one likes a fire ant except another fire ant.

SHAMBO THE TEMPLE MONKEY
(Macaca mulatta)

Shambo will be missed. Who can forget his wild pranks? How many tails did he pull - always pretending innocence? Who doesn't remember when he dropped headfirst from the banyan branch into a fresh pile of elephant dung – then bounded up with an "I meant to do that" somersault into the river?

He wasn't the strongest or smartest macaque in the troop; he had no wives and he left no children. But no one could make others laugh like Shambo. He was the wild card; the one who made things fun even when they weren't supposed to be fun; like when the monsoon never came but the "clean-up the temple" campaigners did. We remember how he followed them, imitating their stiff and silly walks, until we squealed with laughter and they turned, only to find him quietly grooming his ass.

Shambo loved to swim. He could never resist splashing anyone who was dry, or carrying a handful of water to anoint a passerby. Furious, his victim would chase him up the tree and down the tree and across the walk until Shambo jumped into the river and pretended to have been punished. Mollified, the victim turned away and Shambo chose his next target.

He was a tireless playmate – the favorite of every youngster – as gentle with the young ones as their mothers. And what a groomer! Yes, a pinch or a tickle was coming when least expected, but it was worth it because Shambo was so thorough and careful, and knew just where to scratch.

His face was like a clump of leaves in the wind; always changing shape, drooping, pouting, flashing into a grin so wide you had to smile.

His end was like another prank. We watched him roll backward into the river, sit up in bliss, then disappear in a geyser and splash. We waited for the punchline, but it never came - only the tail of a crocodile slicing the water's surface as it cruised away. Donations may be sent to the International Primate Protection League.

BEEZOO THE CLOWNFISH
(Amphiprion percula)

Beezoo was born in the Great Barrier Reef. After hatching, he spent a week as a transparent speck of plankton, chased by tiny minnows and baby squid before settling on the sandy bottom and starting to get his colors. He chose his anemone very carefully, brushing through its tentacles delicately until his whole body was acclimated and he was safe from its sting.

His new home was protected from most outside dangers, but Beezoo shared it with half a dozen larger clownfish who kept him on the run. He was the runt – and the larger fish made sure he stayed that way. No particle of food was uncontested and no nook or cranny was Beezoo's if another clownfish wanted it. He spent most of his time hiding.

As the years went by, Beezoo's neighbors changed. Queen Mabel got reckless and was eaten by an eel, so everyone got a promotion. Beezoo made it all the way to runt first class and finally was getting almost enough to eat. But the larger fish still pestered him and kept him down and out of the way. Only the new Queen (Zia) and the biggest male got to mate, and they treated Beezoo more like food than a member of the family.

Then, when Beezoo was four years old, a typhoon struck the reef and swept away three of the home fish. To his astonishment and relief, he was the largest male left – the only male left, in fact. He doubled in size in a week – wolfing down the plentiful food so he could hold his position if a challenger came along. Three new males did move in, but by then Beezoo was a bruiser and he let them know he was in charge, second only to Queen Zia, of course.

But Queen Zia was getting old. She had taken a beating in the typhoon. She was only able to lay a couple of hundred eggs at a time, which Beezoo fertilized and tended, fanning them often to keep them fresh and lively. And then she died.

Beezoo had made it. He was the top clownfish. He cruised the polyps and received homage from the other males, then hunkered down - for a major change.

When Beezoo died last week at the age of fourteen, she was the mother and grandmother of thousands of clownfish and the queen of her domain. Donations in her honor to the Marine Conservation Institute would be appreciated.

BERNICE THE BIG-EARED BAT
(Corynorhinus townsendii)

Among others, moths and lacewings are safer today – Bernice the Bat is no more. She was found on her back beneath an oak tree early this morning, twitching and trembling, her eyes rolling and watering. Witnesses report that her mouth foamed while her wings thrashed and flapped wildly against the ground. And then she was dead from rabies at the age of seven.

Bernice had raised six pups, three of whom still live in the area. She thoroughly enjoyed mingling with the other mothers in the early summer when they huddled together to give birth and raise their young. She hesitated to leave her young pups when it was time to feed, but nursing mothers need nourishment, so Bernice would leave the cave at night and hunt for insects.

Her huge ears could still hear her baby's squawks for some distance, but then she shifted to sonar and sifted the night for landmarks and flying food. When she detected movement, she often switched to silent running, relying only on her ears to guide her to her prey. She could hear the whisper of a moth antenna or the rustle of wing upon wing. Before day began to break, she was back in her roost, rolling up her precious ears like ram's horns, her belly full of arthropod flesh.

Bernice loved to cuddle – with her babies, her mates, and her sister bats. She was affectionate to all, licking and stroking, savoring the warmth and security of the roost. And so it was hard for her when she began acting strangely and the other bats avoided her touch. Interested parties may wish to honor her memory by supporting the Organization for Bat Conservation.

HOWIE THE HOUSE SPARROW
(Passer domesticus)

Howie died suddenly today at the age of eight, but did he ever pack a lot of living into that short span of time?! He did everything at high speed – and, in the end, it was speed that killed him.

For example: He visited the river bank and two ponds, took a bath in the reservoir, spent several seconds inside a cat's mouth, and lost a couple of feathers to an owl's claw. Then, after flying over the tallest building in the city and through a culvert tunnel beneath the Interstate, he broke into a grocery store, pooped on a church gargoyle, ate fourteen kinds of insects, three kinds of spiders, half a French fry, numerous berries, and thirty-two varieties of seeds. Then he made love seven times with three different females and sat on his life partner's eggs for a total of an hour and a half. He scolded three dogs, one policeman, several pigeons, and hundreds of male sparrows and other small birds. Howie also narrowly avoided collisions with one drone, two bicycles, three taxicabs, and a bus. And all of that was just yesterday morning!

Howie was a "sparrows' sparrow" – he loved to mingle and squabble and bathe with his neighbors. He enjoyed a sing-a-long and began and ended each day with a good chorus. He was a favored mate. Females often fought each other for his attentions and Howie was more than willing to oblige the winners. But he always returned to his partner, Midge, with whom he successfully raised many broods.

Howie often raided people parties – especially outdoor cafes and picnics. Human beings were so incredibly slow and sloppy that he knew their affairs would yield lots of tasty morsels that could be stolen without consequences. He wasn't afraid to gobble crumbs under tables and feet because, no matter how quick the humans were, Howie was always much quicker.

Unfortunately, it was his confidence as a thief among humans that was his undoing. He spotted it just before noon – a sumptuous feast on a sunlit terrace on the fourteenth floor. Howie fluttered above, aimed for the croutons, and dove headfirst – into a plate glass window. Felix the housecat attended to the remains. Friends may wish to celebrate Howie's life by participating in World Sparrow Day activities.

GINA THE GRASS SPIDER
(Agelenopsis sp.)

Yes, she was timid. All you had to do was turn in her direction and Gina was down the hole of her funnel web. But it paid off, didn't it? Braver spiders wound up in the bellies of wasps and birds and salamanders. Gina lived her full cycle.

She was quick. In a flash she was on you; her bite lethal. Her web wasn't sticky, but it was tough to climb out of. And she never missed a vibration. She could sense an aphid's breath if it struck the silken strands.

She was patient, too. She had to be; she had many competitors. On a dewy morning, one could see just how many of her kind had set their silver traps – dotted over the lawns and bushes like giant snowflakes. She often waited for hours or even days for a meal; always ready, always focused on the task at hand.

There were close calls and failures. So many of her webs were trampled and torn by clumsy monsters passing through. Hardest of all to deal with were the tweeners – too small to escape but too big to subdue. Once she let a huge grasshopper tear at her web until he was so entangled he died. It was the only free meal she ever had.

We shouldn't grieve for her; Gina was one of the lucky ones. She found her mate and laid her two egg sacks in a safe place under a fallen locust tree. She guarded them fearlessly – chasing off centipedes and beetles twice her size - but she never saw her offspring. First came the numbing cold and Gina lapsed away peacefully, aged nine months. Two hundred of her youngsters emerged the following spring. A few of them even survived.

Life is a web and Gina spun hers well.

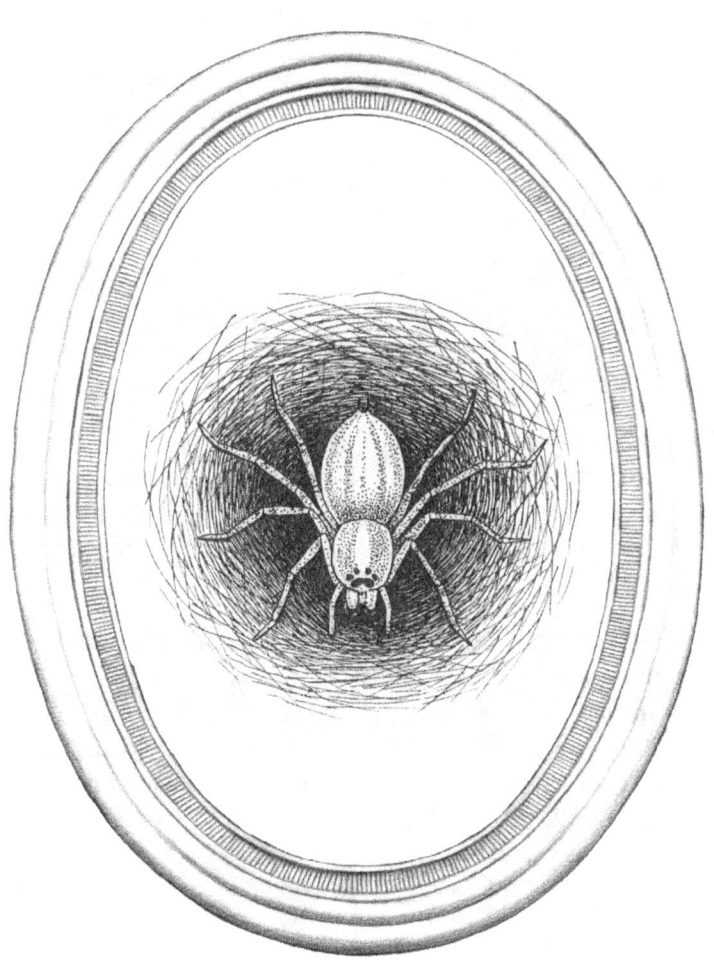

MARIA THE MUSTANG
(Equus ferus caballus)

Died suddenly, yesterday morning at ten o'clock, Maria, aged 18, the wisest and bravest of the herd. The daughter of the late Estrella, Maria was born free on the prairie. She was descended from a mare brought from Spain to the New World in 1586. Maria's father was Apache, alpha stallion, who lived apart from the others and was known for his blinding speed and bad temper.

Maria is survived by seven mares and three stallions, aged 6 months to 16 years. She was with her family in her last moments and died trying to save them from captivity or worse.

On her final day, Maria sensed something was wrong. She raised her head, pricked up her ears and snorted. In the distance seven horses were approaching, each carrying a brightly colored creature with a three-pointed head. The riders cackled like crows and pulled their horses this way and that by their teeth.

Maria reared onto her hind legs, whinnied and ran off, followed closely by the rest of the herd. The creatures followed, hooting and yip-yapping, swinging circles of twine over their heads. The mustangs outpaced them, but as they rounded a corner of the canyon, they faced several more creatures on horseback. The herd balked and buckled, but Maria showed the way. She leapt completely over one horse's rump, tore a gap in the round-up, and raced for open country. The herd followed, trampling one of the creatures who had fallen from his horse.

Though the sky was cloudless and blue as a chicory blossom, there was a crack of thunder - then another. Two lumps of metal whistled into Maria's chest. She reared, pummeled the sky, and crumpled in the dust. Raising her proud black head one last time, she squealed, groaned, and died.

The other members of the herd gathered around Maria, nudging and nibbling, trying to bring her back to life - but in vain. They were soon bullied into their new lives – or deaths. They knew that Maria was the lucky one.

The bereaved may wish to watch "The Path of the Horse" and perhaps make a donation to American Wild Horse Preservation .

DEENA THE MITE
(Demodex folliculorum)

It was a short but pleasant life that came to an end today during an unexpectedly early morning flood. Deena was only 19 days old, but her life had been fruitful and she is survived by hundreds of thriving offspring - and their offspring.

She was born near the Reddish Badlands, just a short crawl from Browntop Mountain and the Upper Forest. It is a region that has been inhabited by her family for well over a thousand generations. The land that Deena inhabited was subject to violent storms and upheavals. There were frequent light flashes of many colors and salty liquids would sometimes well up from beneath the surface. Temperatures could change suddenly and drastically.

Often, after the morning flood, the entire region would be covered by a blizzard of huge smelly boulders of white or bright colors, or inundated with heavy noxious oils or even alcohol. Once during her lifetime, the forest was invaded by huge metal probes that plucked away some of the largest shafts. However, Deena remained snug in her home beneath the surface, only dimly aware of the chaos and clamor above her.

Deena spent every day drinking oil and munching on protein in her subterranean home. Then, when darkness fell after the evening flood, her eight stubby legs would drag her 0.3 millimeter, sock-like body into the fresh air. There were always plenty of males waiting for her to emerge from hiding. After mating, she would waddle into the forest and climb one of the towering trunks. There she would lay her eggs high above the valley floor before returning home ahead of the morning flood. It was a routine that suited Deena well.

This morning, a loud buzzing sound startled Deena as she was making her way home. She had heard the sound before, but only muffled in the safety of her follicle. The buzzing was followed by a heavy flood, hours earlier than usual. Deena tried desperately to hold onto the flaky surface, but the current was too strong and it swept her away into space and a watery gloom. It was the first time she had left the vicinity of the mole beside Judy Wample's eyebrow, and the last.

RINGO THE EARTHWORM
(Lumbricus terrestris)

He/she was the biggest worm in the park. It seemed Ringo would never stop growing - nearly 18 inches long when fully stretched. But death came to Ringo yesterday morning at the age of 14, as it must eventually to all earthworms.

Ringo was a great beneficiary to the community. Of the 12 million annelid inhabitants of tiny Edgewood Park, none converted as much detritus into usable soil as he/she did. His/her deep burrows brought fresh air and water to so many plant roots and tiny animals that it was said you could always find Ringo where the grass was greenest and the birds built their nests.

His/her life was eventful. At the age of nine, Ringo spent half an afternoon in a sweltering bait bucket by the pond before the park ranger convinced a young fisherman to set him/her free. But the most dramatic experience was not suspected by many – Ringo was not born in Edgewood. At the age of two months, a tiny but sufficient piece of Ringo was dropped by a robin flying over the park on its way from across the river. The lost morsel was just a fragment, but enough for him/her to regenerate into a complete worm once again.

Ringo's end came as the result of the recent flooding after a solid week of rain. The soil at the park became so saturated that standing water covered the grass and even parts of the woods. Along with hundreds of thousands of his/her subterranean neighbors, Ringo was forced to flee his/her burrow in pursuit of air to breathe. Thanks to determination and large size, Ringo was able to crawl all the way to the parking lot and stay above the water, but had not the strength to get back to bare earth when the asphalt began to dry.

Mrs. Featherstone chanced upon the carcass Tuesday morning and said a few words on his/her behalf:

"This mighty creature has helped make our park a place of beauty and health. Indeed, Charles Darwin once said 'It may be doubted whether there are many other animals which have played so important a part in the history of the world' as the lowly earthworm."

With that, Mrs. Featherstone lifted the shriveled remains onto the still-wet grass with a stick and went on her way. Several hundred ants and finally a skunk made away with what was left. Friends may wish to scatter a handful of mulch in their gardens as a tribute to Ringo the earthworm.

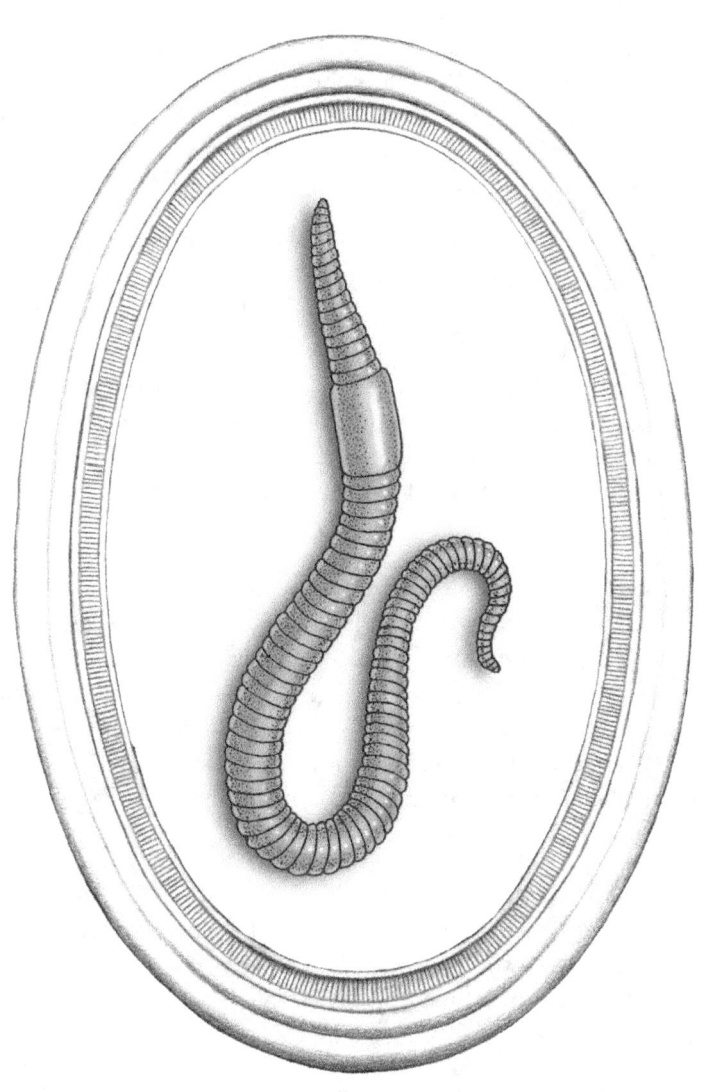

MUKWAH THE GRIZZLY BEAR
(Ursus arctos)

He was an impressive beast to behold: 1350 pounds of solid bear gristle, covered with a heavy cloak of dark brown and golden fur. His sharp, curving claws were at least five inches long – all 17 of them; he lost three while fighting, as well as one eye and several teeth.

In his final hour, Mukwah plopped down sphinx-like at the entrance to his den. Under his heavy fur were hidden a hundred scars; souvenirs of but a fraction of the wars he had won, and the few he had lost. He still carried nearly a pound of buckshot and bullets under his skin. He'd been cut by the teeth and claws of cougars, wolves, coyotes, bears black and brown, wolverines, and a Bowie knife or two. Bison and cow horns had gouged him, and his lips and ears had been stung by thousands of honeybees. But each wound stiffened his flesh and only made him tougher.

When he was thirteen, Mukwah was captured by humans in a barrel trap and put on display at a roadside zoo and diner. He loathed the dogfood they gave him and the stench of gasoline and cigarettes, so after a few weeks, he tore open his cage and made for higher ground. There was a general panic in town – grizzly on the loose! But Mukwah didn't stick around very long. He munched his way through a garden or two, ate Mrs. Thomas's poodle, and climbed the mountain.

There was a bear hunter, Dan Cantrell, who fancied himself a mountain man. "I'll get 'im," he told Mrs. Thomas, and followed Mukwah ever deeper into the forest. It was a favor, really, because Mukwah went farther than he would have, miles beyond the usual campers and feral dogs. Finally Dan caught up with his bear, and lost an arm for his trouble.

The critters in his new territory had to make room for Mukwah. The ground shook when he bounded after an elk or bison calf. Only the hungriest wolf or coyote packs would dare challenge him for a kill, and he never lost a fight if there were fewer than six of them. They would surround him and bare their teeth, but he swiveled and lunged too quickly, and a single claw could bring them down. Mukwah was king of the wild country.

He was 27 years old when he died of wear and tear and old age just now, breathing out one last mighty breath. Soon the wolves and insects will come to take their revenge on his giant corpse, but he won't care. He had his days and they were sweet.

Friends may wish to honor Mukwah's memory by adopting a Grizzly Bear through the World Wildlife Fund.

ROCKY THE RED-BACKED SALAMANDER
(Plethodon cinereus)

Rocky the Salamander died today at the age of 17 as the indirect result of a domestic squabble. He was born no more than six feet from where he died; one of eight siblings who hatched under a decaying oak log. His mother had guarded the eggs diligently – not even leaving the nest to hunt, so she didn't have a decent meal for two months. When Rocky finally emerged, he was less than an inch long, and a lot of that was tail.

He spent most of his youth in the leaf litter between the garden rocks. However, when things got too hot and dry, Rocky was forced to crawl under the rocks where adult salamanders held sway. He was repulsed more than once by the residents, who glared at him, did four-legged push-ups, and nipped at his face and tail. Fortunately, he eventually found refuge in his parents' lair. They recognized his scent and let him stay whenever times were tough.

Finally, Rocky grew large enough to claim his own rock. He slept there in an abandoned wormhole through most of the cold winters and dry hot summers, but he was an active hunter when it was warm and moist. Rocky would aim and fire his tongue at termites and snails and worms and centipedes and pill bugs and you name it. Most of them never knew what hit them.

Life got a lot more complicated for Rocky when he was old enough to mate. Mildred moved in with him when he was five years old. By this time, he was nearly four inches long and in great favor with the neighborhood females. Poor Mildred just about wore herself out chasing away his suitors – without any help from Rocky. Of course, he wouldn't tolerate it when she was approached by other males, so it was constant strife during the mating season.

Rocky was a tough salamander - the survivor of countless struggles with his own kind, plus near fatal combats with a spotted salamander, several toads, and a giant spider. He had lost three legs, two tails, and half a head during his lifetime – and regrown them all in turn. On one occasion, he was even carried across the street by a starling, but managed to escape and find his way home. So Rocky wasn't intimidated when Big George came crashing into his lair last week looking for Mildred.

It was quite a battle. Rocky finally won, but he had sustained a serious injury to his snout, severely impairing his sense of smell. And that was his undoing; he didn't notice the ring-necked snake when it slipped under his rock and grabbed him from behind.

Friends who would like to honor Rocky's memory are urged to make a donation to Save the Salamanders.

SALVATORE THE BROOK TROUT
(*Salvelinus fontinalis*)

Salvatore was a master of stream calculus. He knew all the angles – from top to bottom to sideways; the shortest distance between two moving points. Nothing passed without his noticing. If he couldn't see it, he felt it; if he couldn't feel it, he smelt it.

The stream was like a conveyor belt presenting an endless variety of eating opportunities. Sal let few of them pass without giving them at least a lunge and a strong sniff. If it looked likely, he would charge and gulp it down before another fish had the chance.

Sometimes the prey would pull back. Salvatore couldn't understand how a tiny bug could be so powerful; pulling him through the water, into the air, and onto dry land, where he was poked and prodded and tossed back in the stream. But most of the bugs and minnows did their duty and died.

Who can forget how dapper Sal looked when breeding, with his white-striped fins, red belly, and green flanks speckled with red, yellow, and blue spots. He struggled the first couple of years trying to secure a mate – or fertilize eggs when the male wasn't looking. But then he was four and 12 inches long, and it was Salvatore who had to chase his rivals away. What a frenzy! A dozen males swirling around his female while she prepared her redd and dropped her eggs. Salvatore spun and charged a thousand times to keep them from his prerogatives.

Most of the year, Sal was content just to hang with the gang. The extra eyes watching for threats made up for the friendly nips and nudges. Night or day, he could feel his comrades around him – every twitch and yawn and flutter. Even when they were still, letting the cool, fresh current wash over them, their world was full of sparkle.

Then one day the water changed, turning yellow and cloudy. Salvatore's skin felt funny, as if numb and tingly at the same time. His gills were pumping, but he couldn't catch his breath. The stench and the bitter taste overpowered him, so he let himself be carried downstream, away from the pools and eddies and the trout he knew so well.

It didn't help – the deeper water was just as foul. He began to go blind. He weakened ever more until, swimming belly up, he came to rest with some floating scum and died, aged six. Friends may wish to assist Trout Unlimited in their endeavors to protect the native American Brook Trout and his waters.

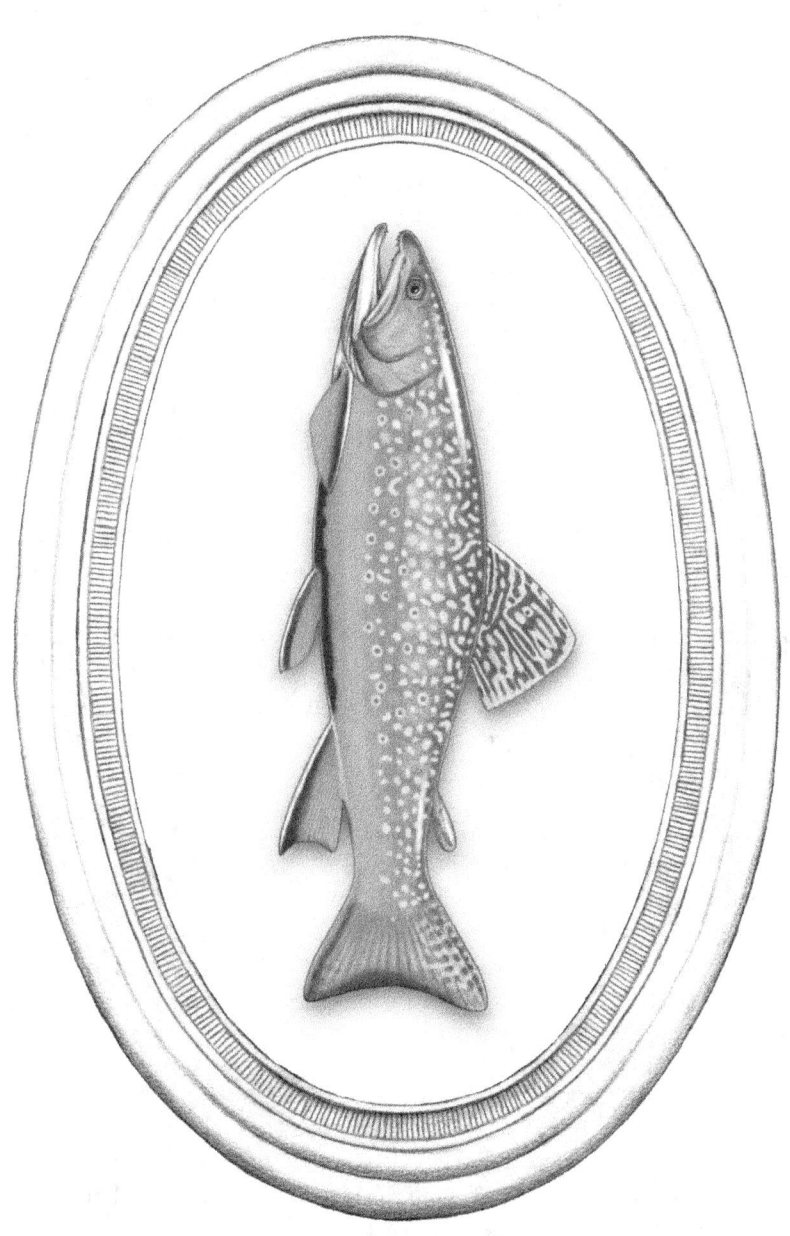

KEENER THE KESTREL
(Falco sparverius)

Do you see that American flag on top of the schoolhouse four blocks away? Can you count the stripes? Maybe not. Keener could count the threads, if he'd wanted to. He could see the ladybug turd between the second and third star on the top row.

First and foremost, he was a good father. During his nine and a half years, Keener raised eight broods of chicks. From the spectacular diving display that won his lifetime partner Kendra, to the tender, patient care he gave her eggs and their nestlings, he was the ideal mate. The chittering and whining of the devoted couple were among the sounds of spring. Twelve of his offspring survive him, plus grandchildren to the seventh generation.

At the beginning of their third season, Keener and Kendra found an ideal nest - a cozy woodpecker hole in an old oak tree. They returned there each spring. Keener brought food to his mate during the weeks prior to and during egg-laying to make sure she was well-nourished. He spent his share of time sitting on the eggs until they hatched. Then he was a tireless provider, bringing in plenty of fresh lizards, rodents, large insects, and small birds to the helpless little balls of fluff until they were fully fledged and ready to fly.

His was a life lived at high speed and high altitude. Keener loved to perch on the highest branch of the highest tree, his huge dark brown eyes catching the tiniest movement below – or above. Even though he usually saw his prey long before it saw him, he was a master of ambush, swooping down out of nowhere with outstretched talons. Many of his victims died of shock even before he tore them open with his powerful, needle-sharp bill.

Last week, Keener returned to the nesting site – only to find that a crow had moved in. He perched on the threshold and let loose a piercing barrage of protests: klee klee klee klee! The crow responded with raucous notes of defiance. Though the black bird was larger than Keener and almost as mean, the brave kestrel barged in and fought bill and claw. It was a bitter struggle and both birds suffered bleeding wounds and lost feathers, but finally the crow moved on.

It was only after he had proclaimed his victory with a long burst of "klees" that Keener realized he had been seriously wounded. The corner of his left eye had been pierced by one of his enemy's talons and he was going blind. Unable to hunt, Keener found a safe perch under a rocky overhang, fluffed out his feathers and waited to die. Kendra brought him food a couple of times, but he refused it. She flew to a nearby tree and kept watch before finally moving on. She will not mate this season.

Keener's friends may offer donations in his name to The Peregrine Fund.

ARTHUR THE PRONGHORN
(Antilocapra americana)

Arthur the Pronghorn was murdered today – shot with an arrow by an assailant who shall remain nameless. Yes, he was a duly licensed hunter, but the circumstances seem to justify a charge of murder.

You see, Arthur was deep into an extended combat with another male pronghorn and understandably preoccupied and oblivious of his surroundings. Taking advantage of this, the hunter let loose a cheap shot. Hunting is a sport, requiring some degree of sportsmanship and fair play. Though not technically a crime, this act dishonors the perpetrator and the sport itself.

Today's incident marked the end of a splendid animal, born nine years, five months, and three days ago. He grew from a wobbly fawn into an 82 inch buck, weighing 130 pounds and sporting 15 inch horns. Who can forget his grace and speed – approaching 60 miles per hour on the open prairie, or his courage when defending his territory or warding off competing suitors. He was as courtly and considerate with does as he was defiant and pugnacious with rival bucks. However, it should be noted that Arthur never attacked another buck when it was engaged in combat.

Arthur is survived by his harem and six generations of descendants, who, no doubt, will miss his leadership and alertness. On many occasions, his exceptional senses of hearing, seeing, and smell allowed him to give the herd early warning of impending danger. How ironic that he should succumb to a rare but understandable lapse.

Friends of Arthur and pronghorns are invited to counsel friends who hunt to behave ethically, respecting their prey and giving them the same fighting chance they would wish to have if they were the hunted. They may also wish to support the Path of the Pronghorn project.

BUSTER THE GHOST CRAB
(Ocypode quadrata)

Man he was fast, scooting sideways on all eight tiptoes! How fast? Ten miles an hour – that's pretty fast when you're six inches wide. He could spin around, change direction, and flash down his hole quicker than a clam can shut his shell.

Buster began his life offshore as a tiny bit of plankton. Life in the sea was a crap shoot and most of his siblings were swallowed up by the jaws all around them. But somehow Buster escaped to grow and change and climb ashore as a bona fide crab.

He was a master builder, tunneling as much as four feet down and sideways, tucking the sand under his right claw and front legs and tossing it away. He'd gently pat the loose sand flat with his claws; to make his home less conspicuous. Then, after a night roaming down the shoreline, Buster would start all over again.

I wish you could have seen him go a-courting. First he faced off against the other males, letting them know where he stood in the pecking order. He and his rivals would bob and weave and strut and preen – holding their powerful claws high in the air, but never touching. Finally one would feel outclassed and withdraw. It was warfare refined – ballet without casualty.

When Buster found a mate, he would spread his claws wide, gripping her delicately as they waltzed along the beach. They'd turn and prance and pirouette. Then he'd invite her into his boudoir, deep in his burrow of cool wet sand. But he would do it in the open, if she preferred. All of her offspring would be his, of course; he always sealed his work when he was done.

Buster turned five last spring and things started going wrong. First he lost his right claw to a seagull who caught him above ground after sunrise. That wasn't too bad - he was left-handed, you see. But he just didn't have the strength to molt and grow a new one. He was wearing out - his legs wore down into nubs. His 360-degree vision fogged over and he was losing his sense of smell.

Buster spent more and more of his time in his burrow, afraid to wander in a world he couldn't see. He'd become slow afoot; he didn't even bother to mate. His tunnels grew shorter and shallower until, last week, a raccoon dug him out and gulped him down. It was a blessing if you ask me – Buster's dancing days were over.

KWANNA THE GRAY FOX
(Urocyon cinereoargenteus)

Yes, she was a curious vixen. Nosey, one might say. Always poking and prying, her eyes darting and her ears swiveling in two directions at once. And it wasn't just about food. Kwanna wanted to know what everything around her was and if it could be eaten or chewed or played with.

She was born eight years ten months ago, one of four kits raised by Mona and Stan. She was tiny and blind at first, confined to the family den under an old stump with her mother and siblings while her father foraged for food. Kwanna was weaned at one month and began to eat solid food. When she was four months, the family began to leave the den and forage together at night and in the twilight.

What fun they had, tumbling through forest and field, frolicking in the river, scurrying up trees and rock piles, learning about their world and how to survive in it. One could hear the six of them, rustling through the leaves in search of salamanders and shrews, or whatever they could find. Kwanna loved to tussle with her sister and brothers, chuckling and squealing as she bit them gently and clawed through their long soft fur. When there was danger, her parents' raspy barks alerted the kits, and they all ran off to safety.

When Kwanna was nine months old, the family broke up and each fox went its own way for the winter. By this time, she was wise to the wilderness and well able to take care of herself, but she was still intrigued by anything unfamiliar or out of reach.

That spring, Kwanna noticed a new scent in her territory. It made her feel giddy and warm inside. Needless to say, she couldn't rest until she found its source. She poked her long nose into every hollow tree and root hole until she found him – Charlie, her life-long mate. They found a home in an abandoned owl's nest high in a dying tulip poplar tree. Kwanna gave birth to three pups that first year – two males and a female – and soon she was part of a frolicking family again. It was the first of seven families that Kwanna and Charlie would raise.

Even when Kwanna was a great times four grandmother, she was still as curious as ever. A couple of weeks ago she discovered a shiny gray contraption by the stream. It had arches and rings and a smelly chunk of meat right in the middle of a flat round plate. There was another smell, too, that Kwanna didn't like very much. It reminded her of those huge white boxes and strange two-legged creatures on the edge of the forest. But she couldn't help herself; she had to know what that meat tasted like.

Friends may make donations in Kwanna's honor to The Wildlife Land Trust. They may also want to encourage the use of humane animal traps.

SOBEK THE NILE CROCODILE
(Crocodylus niloticus)

He was a survivor from another age; a giant, terrifying reptile – truly a latter day dinosaur. And now Sobek, too, is part of the past. He died this morning at the age of 73.

He was born on a sandy lake shore to his devoted mother Mamba on June 14, 1943. After three months of fasting and guarding her nest, she heard the chirps of Sobek and 34 of his siblings and scooped away the top of their nest so they could climb free. She gathered a few un-hatched eggs into her mouth and helped break them open by delicately rolling them between her tongue and the roof of her mouth. Then the baby crocodiles scurried into her jaws and were carried to water, half a dozen at a time.

For two years, Mamba kept watch over her brood, chasing away predators and moving the young crocs to better waters when necessary. Nevertheless, Sobek was one of only five who survived to adolescence. Active mostly at night, he left Mamba and took to the bush in search of insects, snails, toads and frogs – whatever prey he could overpower. He lived more like a lizard than a crocodile, spending much of his time away from water, but the risk of being eaten by larger members of his own kind kept him on dry land.

When he was seven feet long – size matters more than age with crocodiles – he was big enough to join the adults at the lake and switch to eating fish. Sobek soon learned to join the others in blocking the mouth of a stream, forcing schools of fish to run their gauntlet. He was fast – his bite quicker than a viper's strike – and he could swim 20 miles per hour.

Sobek added a foot of length a year and when he was 14, he felt the urge to mate. He battled for territory with the males his size – and fled from those who were larger. One struggle cost him a couple of teeth, but the 64 that remained would be enough. Then he started advertising: bellowing, slapping water with his snout, bubbling through his nose - anything to get attention. Finally, a nine-foot female was impressed. She only laid 22 eggs that year, but Sobek helped guard the nest and hatchlings and all but seven survived their first "two feet".

By the time he was 17 feet long, Sobek was master of all he surveyed. No animal was safe, except perhaps for grown elephants and the largest hippos. He didn't hesitate to attack wildebeests, antelopes, goats, donkeys, chimps – even giraffes and water buffalo. He sank his teeth into their flesh with the strongest bite on the planet and pulled them into deeper water, where they drowned and were torn to pieces by his "death roll".

And then he would do nothing but lay in the sun or moonlight with his mouth agape – for weeks, even months. He wasn't asleep; he saw and heard everything around him. But his meal was enough to last for a year or two, if necessary. Every so often there would be a drought and Sobek would sleep – or rather aestivate; laying still in his underground burrow, his heart beating five times a minute until the rains came again.

His growth slowed in his later years: he finally inched past 20 feet when he was forty and weighed over 2000 pounds. By this time, most of his meals were killed for him by other crocs, or lions, or hyenas, or wild dogs. All he had to do was amble over to a kill and it was his. No one argued with Sobek anymore.

But this morning his vast corpse, slumped and lifeless, was found on the beach. It took several hours before any creature was brave enough to see if he was faking it. He wasn't.

Sobek's passing will be marked by a press conference, parade, and celebration in town. It seems he had eaten around 150 human beings during his lifetime. Unfortunate, but at least they weren't an endangered species. Friends may wish to support the Crocodile Specialist Group.

MAXI THE BEARDED COLLIE MIX
(Canis lupus)

A gloom descended over the neighborhood of West Maple and Pine between 11h and 12th Streets yesterday when word spread that Maxi the bearded collie mix had passed away at the age of 14. She was a familiar figure and friend to most area residents, greeting all she met on her morning and evening walks or while performing her duties as yard security guard and newspaper retriever.

She was born in her family basement on November 12, 2001, the sole female of a litter of five delivered by Trixie, a purebred bearded collie from Connecticut. Maxi's father is believed to have been the golden retriever who belonged to the Caldwells before they moved away, but this was never confirmed. She was named by Carly, the oldest child of Mr. and Mrs. Peters, who called her Maxi because she was the largest of the brood. Maxi is survived by at least 15 offspring, all born before she was fixed at the age of six and a half.

"Maxi was my best, most intimate friend – she was more than just a pet," said Jack Peters, aged 11. "She really was special," added Mrs. Peters. "Whenever someone in the family looked sad or discouraged, Maxi would shamble over and lay her furry chin on that person's knee and gaze with her soulful, sparkling eyes into his or hers. Then the licking would begin – and continue until a walk or a ramble on the rug brought a smile to the person's face." "We'll miss her more than words can say," said Mr. Peters, the tears rolling down his cheeks.

But it was Carly, now a college student, who perhaps said it best: "Maxi was a dog, so she had a different kind of body than the rest of us. But I don't think our bodies are who we really are. Maxi's heart and soul were just as deep and full of magic as yours or mine. We've lost a sister, a true member of the family, and we'll never get over it completely."

Maxi's remains will be interred in the Peters' back yard tomorrow morning. Friends are invited to attend. They may also wish to make a contribution in Maxi's name to their local SPCA.

KANATHWA – THE LAST OF THE MASTODONS
(*Mammut americanum*)

Today marks the anniversary of the passing of Kanathwa, the last mastodon to live in North America. The exact year of her demise is not known for certain - 8500 B.C. is probably a good guess. Her death was a violent one, caused by the massive bleeding that followed the penetration of her flesh and major organs by at least seventeen spear points. However, the circumstances of Kanathwa's death were much more remarkable than its manner implies.

She was the survivor of many hunting raids. She had often heard the staccato shouts and ringing laughter of human hunters as they felled and butchered her companions. Each time, she had escaped – too small to be a primary focus; too old to stay with a fallen parent and be slaughtered for the fun of it. Each time, she had disappeared into the spruce forest for days before searching for and rejoining the shrinking herd.

Six months before the end, Kanathwa began a final search for survivors who did not exist. She ranged far and wide, scouring woods and pasture and water holes – all in vain. There were no mastodons left. She had come of age; she felt the reproductive urge within her – but there was no mastodon bull to give her ease. She was alone. Completely, irrevocably alone.

Kanathwa became frantic. Tears flowed onto her heavy brown fur and dried into green slime. She ran and ran and bellowed until her throat was dry and cracking open, oozing blood. She ran until she heard human laughter.

Kanathwa stumbled to a halt in the frozen grass. Steam rose from her brow. Her vision blurred. Her brain burned with anger. She charged into the hunting camp – crushed three young men underfoot and flung another hard against a tree with her trunk. Then came pain as the sharpened stones tore through her heavy hide and into her core. But the pain was relief; the death was a kindness.

When she passed away, Kanathwa left no relatives to mourn her. Friends may wish to contribute to Save the Elephants in her memory.

EPILOGUE

To end upon a happier note... Premature extinction is not necessary, for either animals or humans. Life has survived many catastrophes in the past 3.8 billion years – collisions with comets and asteroids, the coalescence of continents, global warming and cooling, sea level rising and falling. It will almost certainly survive the ascendancy of mankind.

Animals are more than just food, companionship, competition, and entertainment; animals are our teachers, our friends, our relatives. Their bodies and behaviors mirror our own and they can show us many new and wonderful ways to survive and prosper as a species.

Readers are invited to reflect and remember – to celebrate the lives of animals known and loved in the past. To jot down or imagine obituaries for the pets and wild and domesticated creatures who have enriched and sustained their lives and set examples of beauty, grace, devotion, persistence, ingenuity, and sheer joy. All of these qualities and more have enabled them – and us – to inhabit this planet for so many millions of years.

The next time we encounter an animal – with our eyes, ears, or in our laps – we should ask ourselves: Do I feel superior to this creature? On what basis? Do I apply these standards to other people or to myself? Can I empathize with this being and understand what it feels and how it experiences life in this world? The closer we look at animals, the more we will see ourselves and realize, with both pride and humility, that we are animals, too.

Books by Jasper Burns

Animal Obituaries (Pietas Publications, 2016)

The Necessary Nerd: Essential Stereotypes in the Basic Human Group (Pietas Publications, 2015)

Trice Blessed (Pietas Publications, 2015)

Drawings by Jasper Burns (Pietas Publications, 2014)

Inside (Pietas Publications, 1981, 2014)

P. B.'s Quick Index to Game Fish of the Chesapeake Bay (Pietas Publications, 2014)

Virginia Through Time (Pietas Publications, 2014)

Two Lucys in Europe (Pietas Publications, 2014)

A Lady in Jamaica (Pietas Publications, 2014)

Gale Hill: The Story of an Old Virginia Home (Pietas Publications, 2013)

Ammonite: An Eco-Fantasy (Pietas Publications, 2013)

Coin Stories (Pietas Publications, 2013)

Senior Moments (Pietas Publications, 2013)

Seeing God: Close Encounters of the Divine Kind (Pietas Publications, 2012)

Commodus and the Five Good Emperors (Pietas Publications, 2012)

Turtle Crossing (Pietas Publications, 2012)

Dreamweaving (Pietas Publications, 2012)

Roman Empresses (Pietas Publications, 2012)

Wisdom Illustrated (Pietas Publications, 2012)

Fossil Beach (Pietas Publications, 2012)

Bulla Felix: The Roman Robin Hood (Pietas Publications, 2011)

Irish Hammered Pennies of Edward IV and Richard III (three editions) (Pietas Publications, 2009-15)

Great Women of Imperial Rome: Mothers and Wives of the Caesars (Routledge, 2007)

Fossil Dreams (Pietas Publications, 2007)

Selected Lives: The Autobiography of a Soul (Pietas Publications, 1986, 2006)

Vipsania: A Roman Odyssey (Pietas Publications, 2006)

Trilobites: Common Trilobites of North America (NatureGuide Books, 2000)

Exploring Fossils (Virginia Museum of Natural History, 1998)

Fossil Collecting in the Mid-Atlantic States (Johns Hopkins University Press, 1991)

As Illustrator

Illustrated Field Guide to Congenital Heart Disease and Repair (Scientific Software Solutions, Inc., 2004)

Fun with Mammals, by Nancy D. Moncrief with Sonya Wolen (Virginia Museum of Natural History, 1999)

Frommer's Guide to Yellowstone and Grand Teton National Parks (MacMillan Travel, 1998)

Discovering Fossils, by Frank A. Garcia and Donald S. Miller (Stackpole Books, 1998)

The MINTS Book: Model Inquiries into Nature in the Schoolyard, (Virginia Museum of Nat. History, 1997)

Angling Alpine, by J. E. Warren (Alpine County California Chamber of Commerce, 1993)

P. B.'s Quick Index to Bird Nesting, by Philip A. Burns (published by author, 1983)